N̄
KOWHAI

Published in 1999 by New Holland Kowhai
an imprint of New Holland Publishers (NZ) Ltd
Auckland • Sydney • London • Cape Town

218 Lake Road, Northcote, Auckland, New Zealand
14 Aquatic Drive, Frenchs Forest, NSW 2086, Australia
24 Nutford Place, London W1H 6DQ, United Kingdom
80 McKenzie Street, Cape Town 8001, South Africa

ISBN: 1 877246 19 0

Managing editor: Renée Lang
Book design: Graeme Leather
Colour reproduction by Colour Symphony Pte Ltd
Printed by Craft Print Pte Ltd, Singapore

FRONT COVER: Parapents hover over Queenstown, Lake Wakatipu
and the Remarkables.
BACK COVER, LEFT TO RIGHT:
Courtyard of Gibbston Valley Wines; freestyle skier at
Coronet Peak; river surfers on the Kawarau River; canyoning
at Emerald Stream, near Wanaka.
INSIDE BACK FLAP: The tranquil waters of Lake Hayes.
END PAPERS (FRONT AND BACK): Autumn colours at Arrowtown.
TITLE PAGE: A Shotover jet boat exhilarates passengers with a 360° spin.
OPPOSITE: Queenstown and the Remarkables at dusk.

Introduction

*T*he name Queenstown is synonymous with activities like jet boating, bungy jumping, skiing, parapenting and rafting, and often attracts the label 'adventure capital of the world'. However, a mere label cannot do justice to the Queenstown region.

Glaciers have carved numerous deep lakes and coastal fiords which are separated by snow-capped mountains. Wild rivers have created dramatic canyons, and the vegetation ranges from rainforest to near-desert. Set amidst the stunning scenery, and stemming from the wild days of the goldrush, are historic settlements which today provide visitors with first-class accommodation, restaurants and lively nightlife.

With a unique blend of history, adrenalin-packed adventure and stunning scenery, Queenstown has become an expansive playground for visitors and locals – one of the world's top holiday destinations.

The historic steamship T.S.S. *Earnslaw* pulls out of Queenstown Bay.

LEFT AND RIGHT: High above Queenstown, bungy jumpers leap from 'The Ledge' – one of several bungy sites in the region.

OVERLEAF, LEFT: Late afternoon light falls on the jagged peaks of the Remarkables.

OVERLEAF, RIGHT: The T.S.S. *Earnslaw*, seen here tied up at the Steamer Wharf, on the left, is one of the numerous boats that depart on lake and river excursions from Queenstown Bay.

Walter Peak High Country Farm can be reached from Queenstown by a 12km boat trip or by an arduous road journey that can take several hours. There are regular steamship excursions across Lake Wakatipu to the farm and Walter Peak caters to the tourists with good facilities and live farm displays.

LEFT: The T.S.S. *Earnslaw* has plied Lake Wakatipu since 1912, and still uses its original coal-fired twin steam engines.

RIGHT: Diners enjoy good food at one of Queenstown's award-winning restaurants.

LEFT: From its base station, the Skyline Gondola rises 450 vertical metres to give superb views over Queenstown and Lake Wakatipu.

RIGHT: White-water rafting trips down the Shotover River start in Skippers Canyon and end here, at the Cascade Rapid.

LEFT: Parapents, or paragliders, are a regular sight in the skies above Queenstown.

RIGHT: A giant teddy bear paraglides into Queenstown as part of the fancy-dress competition for Queenstown's annual winter festival.

OVERLEAF, LEFT: This track through Moke Creek is just one of the numerous popular mountain-bike tracks in and around Queenstown.

OVERLEAF, RIGHT: Coronet Peak Road winds its way up to the ski area of the same name, and is also the only access to the notorious road into Skippers Canyon.

LEFT: Skiers are reflected in the windows of Coronet Peak's modern base facilities.

RIGHT: A skier performs his freestyle moves in one of Coronet Peak's many winter competition events.

OVERLEAF, LEFT: Skiers catch a ride on the quad chairlift at Cardrona Alpine Resort.

OVERLEAF, RIGHT: Snowboard slalom racers compete at Cardrona. The resort has a large number of facilities set up specifically for snowboarders.

LEFT: Competitors are dropped off high in the mountains above Lake Wanaka for the annual extreme ski and snowboard competition.

RIGHT: Skiers and snowboarders enjoy lunch at Treble Cone near Wanaka.

ABOVE AND LEFT: The 1865 Cardrona Hotel has changed remarkably little since the days of the goldrush.

LEFT: Adventurous 'canyoners' explore the hidden world of Emerald Stream Canyon, near Wanaka.

RIGHT: An experienced tandem skydiver guides a first-time jumper in to land at Wanaka airport.

LEFT: Exotic trees on the waterfront near Wanaka township add brilliant autumn colour to the fringes of Lake Wanaka.

OVERLEAF, LEFT: A three-dimensional maze and a tilted room are two of the many amusements and illusions that draw large numbers of people to Wanaka's Puzzling World.

OVERLEAF, RIGHT: Buchanan Peaks (centre) and Mt Alta (right) are reflected in the 45km-long glacier-carved Lake Wanaka.

Stuart Landsborough's
PUZZLING WORLD!
Wanaka, New Zealand

9

LEFT: On even-numbered years the normally peaceful air around Wanaka is shattered by the 'Warbirds over Wanaka' airshow. Held at Easter, the airshow attracts around 70,000 visitors.

RIGHT: Climbers from all over New Zealand and from overseas visit Hospital Flat, near Wanaka, for its rock climbing.

ABOVE: Dawn mist lifts off the Clutha River at Albert Town, as kayakers race in the 400km 'Goldrush' multisport event.

RIGHT: Lake Hawea is a glacier-carved lake not far from Lake Wanaka. At one place, called 'the Neck', they are separated by just a kilometre.

OVERLEAF: Tawny coloured tussock and steep ridges dominate the roadside scenery on the Lindis Pass Road.

CROMWELL

The Centre of Attraction

PREVIOUS PAGES, LEFT: When Lake Dunstan was filled in 1992 a new bridge was built to join the old gold-mining town of Bannockburn to the outside world. The small settlement has recently become known for its vineyards.

PREVIOUS PAGES, RIGHT: Ruins from the days of the goldrush are a common sight around Otago's numerous old goldrush towns. This cart and the remains of a miner's hut are at Bendigo.

LEFT: A giant fruit statue at Cromwell indicates the region's major industry – fruit orchards. Recent plantings also include vineyards and olive groves.

RIGHT: Recreational boaters flock to Otago's lakes in summer for fishing, water-skiing and, as seen here on Lake Dunstan, 'biscuiting'.

PREVIOUS PAGES, LEFT: Most of Cromwell's old town centre was flooded when Lake Dunstan was filled in 1992, but a few remnants are still to be found at the edge of the lake.

PREVIOUS PAGES, RIGHT: Morning mist hangs over the Pisa Range and is reflected in Lake Dunstan. The lake was created by a new hydroelectric dam on the Clutha River, 20km downstream at Clyde.

LEFT: On the flats between the mountain ranges and the Clutha River is Earncleugh. The area is particularly known for its orchards, seen here separated by rows of poplar trees.

RIGHT: Exploring old gold-mining trails in the empty ranges and valleys of Central Otago is a popular recreational pursuit – for those with four-wheel drive vehicles!

PREVIOUS PAGES: In autumn, exotic poplar trees give a brilliant golden-yellow reflection in the calm waters of Butchers Dam near Alexandra.

LEFT AND RIGHT: The historic Kawarau suspension bridge was built in 1880. Just over a century later, in 1988, it became the world's first commercial bungy jumping site, pioneered by New Zealander A.J. Hackett.

LEFT: Novices are taught kayaking skills on the Kawarau River, just below the outlet of Lake Wakatipu.

RIGHT: While it's possible to challenge the mighty power of the Kawarau River in a jet boat, raft or kayak, the latest adventure sport is 'river surfing'.

LEFT: Good food and award-winning wines draw in large numbers of patrons for lunch and wine tasting in the courtyard of Gibbston Valley Wines.

RIGHT: New vines join established ones at Chard Farm in Gibbston Valley – an area where many new vineyards are being established.

OVERLEAF, LEFT: The sometimes notorious 'wild west' reputation of Arrowtown during the heady goldrush days is in stark contrast to the quiet and charming historical township of today.

OVERLEAF, RIGHT: Once only found in the wild, deer are now commonly farmed domestically in the southern South Island.

PREVIOUS PAGES: The luxury resort of Millbrook, near Arrowtown, combines world-class facilities (including a championship golf course) and old world charm, in a unique setting surrounded by mountains.

LEFT: A kayaker tests his skills on a fast-flowing rapid in the Kawarau Gorge.

RIGHT: The track into Skippers Canyon was first carved into the steep hills and sheer bluffs in the 1880s. Today the road is still infamous, and companies refuse to insure rental cars on Skippers Road.

LEFT: One of New Zealand's highest bungy jumps, the 102m
Pipeline Bungy is located deep in Skippers Canyon.

RIGHT: Precipitous bluffs and abrupt cliff faces are typical of the terrain in
Skippers Canyon – it is not a place for the faint-hearted.

LEFT: Jet boats were invented by New Zealand farmer Bill Hamilton in the 1950s, and have been used by Shotover Jet for commercial trips since 1964.

RIGHT: A powerful and manoeuvrable jet boat takes passengers on an exhilarating ride as it skims past rock faces in the Lower Shotover Canyon.

ABOVE: Huge rainbow trout, as well as brown trout, eels and ducks, can be seen in their natural habitat from Underwater World on Queenstown Pier. Fishing is banned in Queenstown Bay!

RIGHT: The clear glacier-fed waters of Lake Wakatipu are very deep and very cold – even the hardiest of swimmers last only a few minutes. However, the water at Frankton Beach is shallower and often a few degrees warmer.

At the south end of Lake Wakatipu, between October and April, 'The Kingston Flyer' steam train operates short excursions on a 14km section of track between Kingston and Fairlight.

LEFT: Sunset over the South Island's largest lake – the 61km-long Lake Te Anau – as seen from the township of Te Anau.

RIGHT: Mt Luxmore hut on the Kepler Track gives inspiring views over South Fiord on Lake Te Anau.

LEFT: A runner climbs Mt Luxmore in the 'Kepler Challenge' – an annual 67km mountain race.

RIGHT: The Sutherland Falls and Lake Quill are among the main attractions for trampers walking the world-famous Milford Track.

LEFT: The 32km Routeburn Track is one of New Zealand's most popular tramping tracks. It takes in a variety of landscapes including waterfalls, lakes and alpine scenery, as well as the beech forest seen here.

RIGHT: Trampers cross a footbridge over the Route Burn river near the Glenorchy end of the Routeburn Track.

OVERLEAF, LEFT: A campervan on the Milford Road World Heritage Highway. The road travels along deep, vertically sided, glacier-carved valleys, and through Homer Tunnel. It is the only direct road access to any point on Fiordland's 1000km of remote coastline.

OVERLEAF, RIGHT: The kea, New Zealand's alpine parrot, has an extremely strong beak, a playful and curious nature, and is particularly fond of destroying car door rubber seals and windscreen wipers.

LEFT: Bowen Falls, seen here, is one of just three permanent waterfalls in Milford Sound, although regular heavy rain can lead to dozens of temporary waterfalls cascading down the sheer walls of the Sound.

RIGHT: Milford Sound is the most northern and the most accessible of the 13 major fiords that deeply indent the isolated coastline of Fiordland.

OVERLEAF: Mitre Peak rises straight up from the ocean. Its summit is 1695m vertically above Milford Sound – equivalent to five times the height of the Eiffel Tower or four times that of the Empire State Building.